Beautiful Britain— Cambridge

by

Gordon Home

Beautiful Britain—Cambridge
by Gordon Home

ISBN: 978-93-60468-41-5

Published by

DOUBLE 9 BOOKS

2/13-B, Ansari Road
Daryaganj, New Delhi – 110002
info@double9books.com
www.double9books.com
Tel. 011-40042856

ABOUT THE AUTHOR

Gordon Cochrane Home was an English landscape painter, author, and illustrator who lived from July 25, 1878, until December 13, 1969. London is where Home first appeared. He was employed as an art editor by publishers A & C Black as well as "The Tatler" and "The King." After serving in France and North Africa as a Major in the Royal Army Service Corps from 1914 to 1920, he went on extensive travels throughout North Africa, the British Empire, and the Commonwealth. Home regularly showed at the Royal Academy and focused mostly on watercolor and pen and ink painting. In 1921, he participated in the Society of Graphic Art's inaugural annual exhibition. Home penned and illustrated numerous travel and historical fiction books for companies such as A & C Black and J M Dent.

CONTENTS

CHAPTER I
SOME COMPARISONS

"...and so at noon with Sir Thomas Allen, and Sir Edward Scott and Lord Carlingford, to the Spanish Ambassador's, where I dined the first time.... And here was an Oxford scholar, in a Doctor of Laws' gowne.... And by and by he and I to talk; and the company very merry at my defending Cambridge against Oxford." — PEPYS' *Diary* (May 5, 1669).

In writing of Cambridge, comparison with the great sister university seems almost inevitable, and, since it is so usual to find that Oxford is regarded as pre-eminent on every count, we are tempted to make certain claims for the slightly less ancient university. These claims are an important matter if Cambridge is to hold its rightful position in regard to its architecture, its setting, and its atmosphere. Beginning with the last, we do not hesitate to say that there is a more generally felt atmosphere of repose, such as the mind associates with the best of our cathedral cities, in Cambridge than is to be enjoyed in the bigger and busier university town. This is in part due to Oxford's situation on a great artery leading from the Metropolis to large centres of population in the west; while Cambridge, although it grew up on a Roman road of some importance, is on the verge of the wide fenlands of East Anglia, and, being thus situated off the trade-ways of England, has managed to preserve more of that genial and scholarly repose we would always wish to find in the centres of learning, than has the other university.

Then this atmosphere is little disturbed by the modern accretions to the town. On the east side, it is true, there are new streets of dull and commonplace terraces, which one day an awakened England will wipe out; there are other elements of ugly sordidness, which the lack of a guiding and controlling authority, and the use of distressingly hideous white bricks, has made possible, but it is quite conceivable that a visitor to the town might spend a week of sight-seeing in the place without being aware of these shortcomings. This fortunate circumstance is due to the truly excellent planning of Cambridge. It is not for a moment suggested that the modern growth of the place is ideal, but what is new and unsightly is so placed that it does not interfere with the old and beautiful. The real Cambridge is so effectively girdled with greens and commons, and college grounds shaded with stately limes, elms, and chestnuts, that there are never any jarring backgrounds to destroy the sense of aloofness from the ugly and untidy elements of nineteenth-century individualism which are so often conspicuous at Oxford.

Cambridge has also made better use of her river than has her sister university; she has taken it into her confidence, bridged it in a dozen places, and built her colleges so that the waters mirror some of her most beautiful buildings. Further than this, in the glorious chapel Henry VI. built for King's College, Cambridge possesses one of the three finest Perpendicular chapels in the country—a feature Oxford cannot match, and in the church of the Holy Sepulchre Cambridge boasts the earliest of the four round churches of the Order of the Knights Templars which survive at this day.

But comparisons tend to become odious, and sufficient has been said to vindicate the exquisite charm that Cambridge so lavishly displays.

CHAPTER II
EARLY CAMBRIDGE

Roman Cambridge was probably called Camboritum, but this, like the majority of Roman place names in England, fell into disuse, and the earliest definite reference to the town in post-Roman times gives the name as Grantacaestir. This occurs in Bede's great *Ecclesiastical History*, concluded in A.D. 731, and the incident alluded to in connection with the Roman town throws a clear ray of light upon the ancient site in those unsettled times. It tells how Sexburgh, the abbess of Ely, needing a more permanent coffin for the remains of AEtheldryth, her predecessor in office, sent some of the brothers from the monastery to find such a coffin. Ely being without stone, and surrounded by waterways and marshes, they took a vessel and came in time to an abandoned city, "which, in the language of the English, is called Grantacaestir; and presently, near the city walls, they found a white marble coffin, most beautifully wrought, and neatly covered with a lid of the same sort of stone." That this carved marble sarcophagus was of Roman workmanship there seems no room to doubt, and Professor Skeat regards it as clear that this ruined town, with its walls and its Roman remains, was the same place as the Caer-grant mentioned by the historian, Nennius.

In course of time the Anglo-Saxon people of the district must have overcome their prejudices against living in what had been a Roman city, and Grantacaestir arose out of the ruins of its former greatness. In the ninth century a permanent bridge was built, and the town began to be known as Grantabrycg, or, as the Anglo-Saxon Chronicle gives it, Grantebrycge. Domesday toned this down to Grentebrige, and that was the name of Cambridge when a Norman castle stood beside the grass-grown mound which is all that remains to-day of the Saxon fortress. What caused the change from G to C is hard to discover, but when King John was on the throne the name was written Cantebrige, and the "m" put in its appearance in the earlier half of the fifteenth century, the "t" being discarded at the same period. It seems that the name of the river was arrived at by the same process. Perhaps the oddest feature of the whole of these vicissitudes in nomenclature is the similarity between the Roman Camboritum and

Cambridge, for the two names have, as has been shown, no connection whatsoever.

A map of Cambridgeshire, compiled by the Rev. F.G. Walker, showing the Roman and British roads reveals instantly that the university town has a Roman origin, for it stands at the junction of four roads, or rather where Akeman Street crossed Via Devana, the great Roman way connecting Huntingdon and Colchester. Two or three miles to the south, however, the eye falls on the name of a village called Grantchester, and if we had no archaeology to help us, we would leap to the conclusion that here, and not at Cambridge, was the ancient site mentioned by the earlier chroniclers. And this is precisely what happened. Even recent writers have fallen into the same old mistake in spite of the discovery of Roman remains on the site of the real Roman town, and notwithstanding the fact that the two roads mentioned intersect there. The trouble arose through the alterations in spelling in the name of the village of Granteceta, or, as it often appears in early writings, Gransete, but now that Professor Skeat has given us the results of his careful tracking of the name back to 1080, when it first appears in any record, we see plainly that this village has never had a past of any importance, and that the original name means nothing more than "settlers by the Granta." There is a Roman camp near this village, and a few other discoveries of that period have been made there, but such finds have been made in dozens of places near Cambridge.

It is therefore an established fact that modern Cambridge has been successively British, Roman, Saxon, and Norman, and the original town, situated on the north-western side of the river, has extended across the water and filled the space bounded on three sides by the Cam.

Being on the edge of the Fen Country, where the Conqueror found the toughest opposition to his completed sovereignty in England, the patch of raised ground just outside modern Cambridge was a suitable spot for the erection of a castle, and from here he conducted his operations against the English, who held out under Hereward the Wake on the Isle of Ely. In the hurried operations preceding the taking of the "Camp of Refuge" in 1071, there was probably only sufficient time to strengthen the earthworks and to build stockades, but soon afterwards William erected a permanent castle of stone on this marsh frontier—a building Fuller describes as a "stately structure anciently the ornament of Cambridge." In her scholarly work on the town, Miss Tuker tells us how Edward III. quarried the castle to build King's Hall; how Henry VI. allowed more stone to be taken for King's College Chapel; and how Mary in 1557 completed the wiping out of the Norman fortress by granting to Sir Robert Huddleston permission to carry away the remaining stone to build himself a house at Sawston! Wherever building materials are scarce such things have happened, even to the extent of utilizing the stones of stately ruins for road-making purposes. It thus comes about that the artificial mound and the earthworks on the north side of it are as bare and grass-grown as any pre-historic fort which has not at any period known a permanent edifice.

Owing to its fairs, and particularly to the famous Stourbridge Fair, an annual mart of very great if uncertain antiquity, held near the town during September, Cambridge at an early date became a centre of commerce, and it had risen to be a fairly large town of some importance before the Conquest. In the time of Ethelred a royal mint had been established there, and it appears to have recovered rapidly after its destruction by Robert Curthose in 1088, for it continued to be a mint under the Plantagenets, and even as late as Henry VI. money was coined in the town.

A bridge, as already stated, was built at Cambridge in the ninth century, but in 870, and again in 1010, the Danes sacked the town, and it would seem that the bridge was destroyed, for early in the twelfth century we find a reference to the ferry being definitely fixed at Cambridge, and that before that time it had been "a vagrant," passengers crossing anywhere that seemed most convenient. This fixing of the ferry, and various favours bestowed by Henry I., resulted in an immediate growth of prosperity, and the change was recognized by certain Jews who took up their quarters in the town and were, it is interesting to hear, of such "civil carriage" that they incurred little of the spite and hatred so universally prevalent against them in the Middle Ages. The trade guilds of Cambridge were founded before the Conquest, and, becoming in course of time possessed of wealth and influence, some of them were enabled to found a college.

As England settled down under the Norman Kings, the great Abbey of Ely waxed stronger and wealthier, and in the wide Fen Country there also grew up the abbeys of Peterborough, Crowland, Thorney, and Ramsey—all under the Benedictine rules. To the proximity of these great monasteries was due the beginning of the scholastic element in Cambridge, and perhaps the immense popularity of Stourbridge Fair, which Defoe thought the greatest in Europe, may have helped to locate the University there. Exactly when or how the first little centre of learning was established in the town is still a matter of uncertainty, but there seems to have been some strong influence emanating from the Continent in the twelfth century which encouraged the idea of establishing monastic schools. Cambridge in quite early times began to be sprinkled with small colonies of canons and friars, and in these religious hostels the young monks from the surrounding abbeys were educated. Mr. A.H. Thompson, in his *Cambridge and its Colleges*, suggests that the unhealthy dampness of the fens would have made it very desirable that the less robust of the youths who were training for the cloistered life in the abbeys of East Anglia should be transferred to the drier and healthier town, where the learning of France was available among the many different religious Orders represented there.

In 1284 the first college was founded on an academic basis. This was Peterhouse. Its founder was Hugh de Balsham, Bishop of Ely, who had made the experiment of grafting secular scholars among the canons of St. John's Hospital, afterwards the college. Finding it difficult to reconcile the difficulties which arose between secular and religious, he transferred his lay scholars, or Ely clerks, to two hostels at the opposite end of the town, and at his death left 300 marks to build a hall where they could meet and dine. After this beginning there were no imitators until forty years had elapsed, but then colleges began to spring up rapidly. In 1324 Michael House was founded, and following it came six more in quick succession: Clare in 1326, King's Hall in 1337, Pembroke in 1347, Gonville Hall in 1348, Trinity Hall in 1350, and Corpus Christi in 1352. These constitute the first period of college-founding, separated from the succeeding by nearly a century.

The second period began in 1441 with King's, and ended with St. John's in 1509. After an interval of thirty-three years the third period commenced with Magdalene, and concluded with Sidney Sussex in 1595. A fourth group is composed of the half-dozen colleges belonging to last century.

CHAPTER III
THE GREATER COLLEGES

St. John's.—With its three successive courts and their beautiful gateways of mellowed red brick, St. John's is very reminiscent of Hampton Court. Both belong to the Tudor period, and both have undergone restorations and have buildings of stone added in a much later and entirely different style. Across the river stands the fourth court linked with the earlier buildings by the exceedingly beautiful "Bridge of Sighs."

To learn the story of the building of St. John's is a simple matter, for the first court we enter is the earliest, and those that succeed stand in chronological order,—eliminating, of course, Sir Gilbert Scott's chapel and the alterations of an obviously later period than the courts as a whole.

To Lady Margaret Beaufort, the foundress of the college, or, more accurately, to her executor, adviser and confessor, John Fisher, Bishop of Rochester, who carried out her wishes, we owe the first court, with its stately gateway of red brick and stone. It was built between 1511 and 1520 on the site of St. John's Hospital of Black Canons, suppressed as early as 1509.

The second court, also possessing a beautiful gate tower, was added between 1595 and 1620, the expense being mainly borne by Mary Cavendish, Countess of Shrewsbury, whose statue adorns the gateway. Filling the space between the second court and the river comes the third, begun in 1623, when John Williams, then Lord Keeper and Bishop of Lincoln, and afterwards Archbishop of York, gave money for erecting the library whose bay window, projecting into the silent waters of the Cam, takes a high place among the architectural treasures of Cambridge. If anyone carries a solitary date in his head after a visit to the University it is almost sure to be 1624, the year of the building of this library, for the figures stand out boldly above the Gothic window just mentioned. The remaining sides of the third court were built through the generosity of various benefactors, and then came a long pause, for it was not until after the first quarter of the nineteenth century had elapsed that the college was extended to the other side of the river. This new court came into existence, together with the delightful "Bridge of Sighs," between the years 1826 and 1831, when Thomas Rickman, an architect whose lectures and published treatises had given him a wide reputation, was entrusted with the work. The new buildings were not an artistic success, in spite of the elaborate Gothic cloister, with its stupendous gateway and the imposing scale of the whole pile. Their deficiencies might be masked or at least diminished if ivy were allowed to cover the unpleasing wall spaces, and perhaps if these lines are ever read by the proper authority such a simple and inexpensive but highly desirable improvement will come to pass.

The stranger approaching St. John's College for the first time might be easily pardoned for mistaking the chapel for a parish church, and those familiar with the buildings cannot by any mental process feel that the aggressive bulk of Sir Gilbert Scott's ill-conceived edifice is anything but a crude invasion. More than half a century has passed since this great chapel replaced the Tudor building which had unluckily come to be regarded as inadequate, but the ponderous Early Decorated tower is scarcely less of an intrusion than when its masonry stood forth in all its garish whiteness against the time-worn brick of Lady Margaret Beaufort's court. A Perpendicular tower would have added a culminating and satisfying feature to the whole cluster of courts, and by this time would have been so toned down by the action of weather that it would have fallen into place as naturally as the Tudor Gothic of the Houses of Parliament has done in relation to Westminster Abbey. Like Truro Cathedral, and other modern buildings imitating the Early English style, the interior is more successful than the exterior; the light, subdued and enriched by passing through the stained glass of the large west window (by Clayton and Bell) and others of less merit, tones down the appearance of newness and gives to the masonry of 1869 a suggestion of the glamour of the Middle Ages. Fortunately, some of the stalls with their "miserere" seats were preserved when the former chapel was taken down, and these, with an Early English piscina, are now in the chancel of the modern building. The Tudor Gothic altar tomb of one of Lady Margaret's executors—Hugh Ashton, Archdeacon of York—has also been preserved.

At the same time as the chapel was rebuilt, Sir Gilbert Scott rebuilt parts of the first and second courts. He demolished the Master's Lodge, added two bays to the Hall in keeping with the other parts of the structure, and built a new staircase and lobby for the Combination Room, which is considered without a rival in Cambridge or Oxford. It is a long panelled room occupying all the upper floor of the north side of the second court and with its richly ornamented plaster ceiling, its long row of windows looking into the beautiful Elizabethan court, its portraits of certain of the college's distinguished sons in solemn gold frames, it would be hard to find more pleasing surroundings for the leisured discussion of subjects which the fellows find in keeping with their after-dinner port. There is an inner room at one end, and continuing in the same line and opening into it, so that a gallery of great length is formed, is the splendid library, built nearly three centuries ago and unchanged in the passing of all those years.

The library of St. John's is rich in examples of early printing by Caxton and others whose books come under the heading of incunabula, but it would have been vastly richer in such early literature had Bishop Fisher's splendid collection—"the notablest library of books in all England, two long galleries full"—been allowed to come where the good prelate had intended. When he was deprived, attainted, and finally beheaded in 1535 for refusing to accept Henry as supreme head of the Church, his library was confiscated, and what became of it I do not know. Over the high table in the hall, a long and rather narrow structure with a dim light owing to its dark panelling, hangs a portrait of Lady Margaret Beaufort, the foundress of the college, and on either side of this pale Tudor lady are paintings of Archbishop Williams, who built the library, and Sir Ralph Hare. The most interesting portraits are, however, in the master's lodge, rebuilt by Sir Gilbert Scott on a new site north of the library.

It was through no sudden or isolated emotion that Lady Margaret was led to found this college in 1509, the year of her death, for she had four years earlier re-established the languishing grammar college, called God's House, under the new name of Christ's College, and had been a benefactress to Oxford as well. On the outer gateways of both her colleges, therefore, we see the great antelopes of the Beauforts supporting the arms of Lady Margaret, with her emblem, the daisy, forming a background. Sprinkled freely over the buildings, too, are the Tudor rose and the Beaufort portcullis.

St. John's Hospital, which stood on the site of the present college, had been founded in 1135, and was suppressed in 1509, when it had shrunk to possessing two brethren only. The interest of this small foundation of Black Canons would have been small had it not been attached to Ely, and through that connection made the basis of Bishop Balsham's historic experiment already mentioned.

The founding of St. John's by a lady of even such distinction as the mother of Henry VII. could not alone have placed the college in the position it now occupies: such a consummation could only have been brought about by the capacity and learning of those to whom has successively fallen the task of carrying out her wishes, from Bishop Fisher down to the present time. To mention all, or even the chief, of these rulers of the college is not possible here, and before saying farewell to the lovely old courts, we have only space to mention that among the famous students were Thomas Wentworth, Earl of Strafford, Lord-Lieutenant of Ireland; Matthew Prior, the poet-statesman; William Wilberforce, and William Wordsworth.

KING'S COLLEGE.—Henry VI. was only twenty when, in 1441, he founded King's College. In that year the pious young Sovereign himself laid the foundation stone, and five years later it is believed that he performed the same ceremony in relation to the chapel, which grew to perfection so slowly that it was not until 1515 that the structure had assumed its present stately form.

It was Henry's plan to associate his college at Eton, which he founded at the same time, with King's. The school he had established under the shadow of his palace at Windsor was to be the nursery for his foundation at Cambridge in the same fashion as William of Wykeham had connected Winchester and New College, Oxford. Henry's first plan was for a smaller college than the splendid foundation he afterwards began to achieve with the endowments obtained from the recently-suppressed alien monasteries. Had the young King's reign been peaceful, there is little doubt that a complete college carried out on such magnificent lines as the chapel would have come into being; but Henry became involved in a disastrous civil war, and his ambitious plans for a great quadrangle and cloister, three other courts, one on the opposite side of the river connected with a covered bridge and an imposing gate tower as well, never came to fruition. Fortunately, Henry's successor, anxious to be called the founder of the college, subscribed towards the continuance of the chapel, but he also diverted (a mild expression for robbery) a large part of Henry's endowments. Richard III., in his brief reign, found time to contribute £700 to the college, but it was not until the very end of the next reign that Henry VII., in 1508, devoted the first of two sums of £5,000 to the chapel, so that the work of finishing the building could go forward to its completion, which took place in 1515.

At the present time the chapel is on the north side of the college, but when originally planned it stood on the south, for the single court which was built is now incorporated in the University Library, and the existing buildings, all comparatively modern, stand in somewhat disjointed fashion to the south, and extend from King's Parade down to the river. Fellows' Building, the isolated block running north and south between the chapel and this long perspective of bastard Gothic, was designed by Gibbs in the first quarter of the eighteenth century, and its severe lines, broken by an open archway in the centre, are a remarkable contrast to the graceful detail, of the chapel. Framed by the great arch, there is a delicious peep of smooth lawn sloping slightly to the river, with a forest-like background beyond.

In the other buildings of King's it is hard to find any interest, for the crude Gothic of William Wilkins, even when we remember that he designed the National Gallery, St. George's Hospital, and other landmarks of London, is altogether depressing. Even the big hall, presided over by a portrait of Sir Robert Walpole, is unsatisfying. It is the custom to scoff at the gateway and stone arcading Wilkins afterwards threw across the fourth side of the grassy court of the college; but, although its crocketed finials are curious, and we wonder at the lack of resource which led to such a mass of unwarranted ornament, it is not aggressive, neither does it jar with the academic repose of King's Parade.

Owing to the extreme uniformity of the exterior of the chapel the eye seems to take in all there is to see in one sweeping vision, refusing subconsciously to look individually at each of the twelve identical bays, each with its vast window of regularly repeated design. But there are some things it would be a pity to pass over, for to do so would be to fail to appreciate the profound skill of the mediaeval architects and craftsmen who could rear a marvellous stone roof upon walls so largely composed of glass. In this building, like its only two rivals in the world—St. George's Chapel at Windsor Castle and Henry VII.'s Chapel at Westminster—the wall space between the windows has shrunk to the absolute minimum; in fact, nothing is left beyond the bare width required for the buttresses, and to build those reinforcements with sufficient strength to take the thrust of a vaulted stone roof must have required consummate capacity and skill. At Eton, where, however, the stone roof was never built, the buttresses planned to carry it appear so enormous that the building seems to be all buttress, but here such an impression could never for a moment be gained, for the chapel filling each bay completely masks the widest portion of the adjoining buttresses. The upper portions are so admirably proportioned that they taper up to a comparatively slight finial with the most perfect gradations.

Directly we enter the chapel our eyes are raised to look at the roof which necessitated that stately row of buttresses, but for a time it is hard to think of anything but the splendour of colour and detail in this vast aisleless nave, and we think of what Henry's college might have been had the whole plan been carried out in keeping with this perfect work. Wordsworth's familiar lines present themselves as more fitting than prose to describe this consummation of the pain and struggle of generations of workers since the dawn of Gothic on English soil:

> Tax not the royal Saint with vain expense,
> With ill-matched aims the architect who planned—
> Albeit labouring for a scanty band
> Of white-robed Scholars only—this immense

> And glorious work of fine intelligence!
> Give all thou canst; high heaven rejects the lore
> Of nicely-calculated less or more;
> So deemed the man who fashioned for the sense
> These lofty pillars, spread that branching roof
> Self-poised, and scooped into ten thousand cells,
> Where light and shade repose, where music dwells
> Lingering—and wandering on as loth to die;
> Like thoughts whose very sweetness yieldeth proof
> That they were born for immortality.

When the sunlight falls athwart the great windows the tracery and the moulded stonework on either side are painted with "the soft chequerings" of rainbow hues, and the magnificent glass shows at its best all its marvellously fine detail, as well as the beauty of its colour. The whole range of twenty-six windows having been executed under two contracts, dated 1516 and 1526, there was opportunity for carrying out a great subject scheme, and thus it was found possible to illustrate practically the whole Gospel story, culminating in the Crucifixion in the east window, and continuing into apostolic times until the death of the Virgin Mary. At the west end is the one modern window. It represents the Last Judgement. It is safe to say that of their period this glorious set of windows has no real rival, and it is hardly possible to do them any justice if the visitor has become a little jaded with sight-seeing. In one of the windows there is a splendidly drawn three-masted ship of the period (Henry VIII.'s reign), high in the bow and stern, with her long-boat in the water amidships, and every detail of the rigging so clearly shown that the artist must have drawn it from a vessel in the Low Countries or some English port. It is one of the best representations of a ship of the period extant. This is merely an indication of the vivid archaeological interest of the glass, apart from its beauty in the wonderful setting of fan vaulting and tall, gracefully moulded shafts.

The splendid oaken screen across the choir, dividing the chapel into almost equal portions, was put up in 1536, at the same time as nearly the whole of the stalls. It is rather startling to see the monogram of Henry VIII. and Anne Boleyn, entwined with true lovers' knots, on this wonderful piece of Renaissance woodwork, for in 1536, the date of the screen, Anne, charged with unfaithfulness, went to the scaffold. How was it, we wonder, that these initials were never removed? The screen also reminds us of the changes in architecture and religion which had swept over England between the laying of the foundation stone and the completion of the internal fittings, for, not only had the Gothic order come to its greatest perfection in this building, and then its whole traditions been abandoned and a reversion to classic forms taken place, but the very religion for which the chapel had been built had been swept away by the Reformation.

The Tudor rose and portcullis frequently repeated within and without the chapel constantly remind us of the important part Henry VII. played in the creation of one of the chiefest flowers of the Gothic order and the architectural triumph of Cambridge.

TRINITY COLLEGE.—Oxford does not possess so large a foundation as Trinity College, and the spaciousness of the great court impresses the stranger as something altogether exceptional in collegiate buildings, but, like the British Constitution, this largest of the colleges only assumed its present appearance after many changes, including the disruptive one brought about by Henry VIII. In that masterful manner of his the destroyer of monasticism, having determined to establish a new college in Cambridge, dissolved not only King's Hall and Michael House, two of the earliest foundations, but seven small university hostels as well. The two old colleges were obliged to surrender their charters as well as their buildings; the lane separating them was closed, and then, with considerable revenues obtained from suppressed monasteries, Henry proceeded to found his great college dedicated to the Trinity.

There is something in the broad and spacious atmosphere of the Great Court suggestive of the change from the narrow and cramped thought of pre-Reformation times to the age when a healthy expansion of ideas was coming like a fresh breeze upon the mists which had obscured men's visions. But even as the Reformation did not at once sweep away all traces of monasticism, so Henry's new college retained for a considerable time certain of the buildings of the two old foundations which were afterwards demolished or rebuilt to fit in with the scheme of a great open court. Thus it was not until the mastership of Thomas Nevile that King Edward's gate tower was reconstructed in its present position west of the chapel. On this gate, beneath the somewhat disfiguring clock, is the statue of Edward III., regarded as a work of the period of Edward IV.

Shortly before Henry made such drastic changes, King's Hall had been enlarged and had built itself a fine gateway of red brick with stone dressings, and this was made the chief entrance to the college. The upper part and the statue of Henry VIII. on the outer face were added by Nevile between 1593 and 1615, but otherwise, the gateway is nearly a whole century earlier.

It is interesting to read the founder's words in regard to the aims of his new college, for in them we seem to feel his wish to establish an institution capable in some measure of filling the gap caused by the suppression of so many homes of learning in England. Trinity was to be established for "the development and perpetuation of religion" and for "the cultivation of wholesome study in all departments of learning, knowledge of languages, the education of youth in piety, virtue, self-restraint and knowledge; charity towards the poor, and relief of the afflicted and distressed."

To the right on entering the great gateway is the chapel, a late Tudor building begun by Queen Mary and finished by her sister Elizabeth about the year 1567. The exterior is quite mediaeval, and all the internal woodwork, including the great *baldachino* of gilded oak, the stalls and the organ screen dividing the chapel into two, dates from the beginning of the eighteenth century. In the ante-chapel the memory of some of the college's most distinguished sons is perpetuated in white marble. Among them we see Macaulay and Newton, whose rooms were between the great gate and the chapel, Tennyson, Whewell—the master who built the courts bearing his name, was active in revising the college statutes, and died in 1866—Newton, Bacon, Wordsworth and others.

On the west side of the court, beginning at the northern end, we find ourselves in front of the Lodge, which is the residence of the Master of the College. The public are unable to see the fine interior with its beautiful dining- and drawing-rooms and the interesting collection of college portraits hanging there, but they can see the famous oriel window built in 1843 with a contribution of £1,000 from Alexander Beresford-Hope. This sum, however, even with £250 from Whewell, who had just been elected to the mastership, did not cover the cost, and the fellows had to make up the deficit. It was suggested that Whewell might have contributed more had not his wife dissuaded him, and a fellow wrote a parody of "The House that Jack Built" which culminated in this verse:

> This is the architect who is rather a muff,
> Who bamboozled those seniors that cut up so rough,
> When they saw the inscription, or rather the puff,
> Placed by the master so rude and so gruff,
> Who married the maid so Tory and tough,
> And lived in the house that Hope built.

The Latin inscription, omitting any reference to the part the fellows took in building the oriel, may still be read on the window.

In the centre of this side of the court is a doorway approached by a flight of steps, and, from the passage to which this leads, we enter the Hall. It was built in the first decade of the seventeenth century, and the screen over the entrance with the musicians' gallery behind belongs to that period.

Unfortunately, the panelling along the sides has replaced the old woodwork in recent times. This beautiful refectory resembles in many ways the Middle Temple Hall in London. The measurements are similar, it has bay windows projecting at either end of the high table, a minstrels' gallery at the opposite end, and well into the last century was heated by a great charcoal brazier in the centre. The fumes found their way into every corner of the hall before reaching their outlet in the lantern. Among the numerous portraits on the walls there are several of famous men. Among them we find Dryden, Vaughan, Thompson (by Herkomer), the Duke of Gloucester (by Sir Joshua Reynolds), Coke (the great lawyer), Thackeray, Tennyson (by G.F. Watts), Cowley and Bentley. On the other side of the entrance passage are the kitchens with the combination rooms above, where more notable portraits hang. The remainder of the court is composed of living-rooms broken by the Queen's Gate, a fine tower built in 1597 facing King Edward's Gate. It has a statue of Elizabeth in a niche and the arms of Nevile and Archbishop Whitgift.

Nevile's Court is approached by the passage giving entrance to the hall. The eastern half was built when Nevile was master between 1593 and 1615, and the library designed by Sir Christopher Wren occupies the river frontage. To the casual observer this building is a comparatively commonplace one, built in two stories, but although it allows space for the arcaded cloister to go beneath it, the library above consists of one floor and the interior does not in the least follow the external lines. On great occasions Nevile's Court is turned into a most attractive semi-open-air ball or reception room. One memorable occasion was when the late King Edward, shortly after his marriage, was entertained with his beautiful young bride at a ball given at his old college.

Passing out of the court to the lovely riverside lawns, shaded by tall elms and chestnuts, we experience the ever-fresh thrill of the Cambridge "Backs," and, crossing Trinity Bridge, walk down the stately avenue leading away from the river with glimpses of the colleges seen through the trees so full of suggestive beauty as to belong almost to a city of dreams.

There are other courts belonging to Trinity, including two gloomy ones of recent times on the opposite side of Trinity Street, but there is, alas! no space left to tell of their many associations.

CHAPTER IV
THE LESSER COLLEGES

PETERHOUSE.—Taking the smaller colleges in the order of their founding, we come first of all to Peterhouse, already mentioned more than once in these pages on account of its antiquity, so that it is only necessary to recall the fact that Hugh de Balsham, Bishop of Ely, founded this the first regular college in 1284. Of the original buildings of the little hostel nothing remains, and the quadrangle was not commenced until 1424, but the tragedy which befell the college took place in the second half of the eighteenth century, when James Essex, who built the dreary west front of Emmanuel, was turned loose in the court. His hand was fortunately stayed before he had touched the garden side of the southern wing, and the picturesque range of fifteenth-century buildings, including the hall and combination room, remains one of the most pleasing survivals of mediaeval architecture in Cambridge.

Dr. Andrew Perne, also known as "Old Andrew Turncoat," and other names revealing his willingness to fall in with the prevailing religious ideas of the hour, was made Master of Peterhouse in 1554, and subsequently he became Vice-Chancellor of the University. He added to the library the extension which now overlooks Trumpington Street, and to him the town is largely indebted for those little runnels of sparkling water to be seen flowing along by the curbstones of some of the streets. The chapel was added in 1632 by Bishop Matthew Wren in the Italian Gothic style then prevalent, and its dark panelled interior is chiefly noted for its Flemish east window. The glass was taken out and hidden in the Commonwealth period, and replaced when the wave of Puritanism had spent itself. All the other windows are later work by Professor Aimmuller of Munich. Before this chapel was built the little parish church of St. Peter, which stood on the site of the present St. Mary the Less, supplied the students with all they needed in this direction.

CLARE.—Michael House, the second college, was, as we have seen, swept away to make room for Trinity, so that the second in order of antiquity is Clare College, whose classic facade of great regularity, with the graceful little stone bridge spanning the river, is one of the most familiar features of the "Backs." The actual date of the founding of the college by Elizabeth de Burgh, daughter of Gilbert de Clare, was 1342, and the court, then built in the prevalent Decorated style, continued in use until 1525, when it was so badly damaged by fire that a new building was decided upon, but the work was postponed until 1635, and was only finished in the second year of the Restoration. Although no shred of evidence exists as to the architect, tradition points to Inigo Jones, whose death took place, however, in 1652. The bridge is coeval with the earliest side of the court, having been finished in 1640. In the hall, marred by great sheets of plate-glass in the windows, there are portraits of Hugh Latimer, Thomas Cecil (Earl of Exeter), Elizabeth de Clare (foundress), and other notable men.

PEMBROKE.—Like Clare, Pembroke College was founded by a woman. She was Marie de St. Paul, daughter of Guy de Chatillon, and on her mother's side was a great-granddaughter of Henry III. She was also the widow of Aymer de Valance, Earl of Pembroke, whose splendid tomb is a conspicuous feature of the Sanctuary in Westminster Abbey.

Instead of the usual modest beginning with one or two existing hostels adapted for the purposes of a purely academic society, the foundress cleared away the hostels on the site nearly opposite historic Peterhouse, and began a regular quadrangle, the first of the non-religious type Cambridge had known. An existing hostel formed one side, but the others were all erected for the special purpose of the college. A hall and kitchen were built to the east, and on the street side opposite was a gateway placed between students' rooms. Marie de St. Paul also received permission from two successive Avignonese Popes to build a chapel with a bell tower at the north-west corner of the quadrangle, and to some extent these exist to-day, incorporated in the reference library and an adjoining lecture-room. Of the other buildings to be seen at the present time the oldest is the Ivy Court, dating from 1633 to 1659. Since then architect has succeeded architect, from Sir Christopher Wren, who built a new chapel in 1667, to Mr. G.G. Scott, the designer of the most easterly buildings in the style of the French Renaissance. Between these comes the street front by Waterhouse, for whose unpleasing façade no one seems to have a good word. There has indeed been such frequent rebuilding at Pembroke that the glamour of association has been to a great extent swept away. This is doubly sad in view of the long list of distinguished names associated with the foundation. Among them are found Thomas Rotherham, Archbishop of York, who was Master of Pembroke; Foxe, the great Bishop of Winchester and patron of learning; Ridley; Grindal, afterwards Archbishop of Canterbury; Matthew Hutton and Whitgift. Beside these masters Edmund Spenser, the poet Gray, and William Pitt are names of which Pembroke will always be proud.

CAIUS.—In the year following the founding of Pembroke Edmund de Gonville added another society to those already established. This was in

1348, but three years later the good man died and left the carrying on of his college to William Bateman, Bishop of Norwich, who had just founded Trinity Hall. He found it convenient to transfer Gonville's foundation to a site opposite his own college, and from this time until the famous Dr. Caius (Kayes or Keyes) reformed it in 1557, the college was known as Gonville Hall.

The buildings now comprise three courts, the largest called Tree Court, being to the east, and the two smaller called Gonville and Caius respectively, to the west side, separated from Trinity Hall by a narrow lane. Tree Court had been partly built in Jacobean times by Dr. Perse, whose monument can be seen in the chapel; but in 1867 Mr. Waterhouse was given the task of rebuilding the greater part of the quadrangle. He decided on the style of the French Renaissance, and struck the most stridently discordant note in the whole of the architecture of the colleges. The tall-turreted frontage suggests nothing so much as the municipal offices of a flourishing borough. The present hall, built by Salvin in 1854, was decorated and repanelled by Edward Warren in 1909. Two of the three curiously named gateways built by Dr. Caius still survive, and one of them, the Gate of Honour, opening on to Senate House Passage, is one of the most delightful things in Cambridge. Dr. Caius had been a Fellow of Gonville Hall, and, having taken up medicine, continued his studies at the University of Padua; and after considerable European travel practised in England with such success that he was appointed Physician to the Court of Edward VI. Philip and Mary showed him great favour, and his reputation grew owing to his success in treating the sweating sickness. Having acquired much wealth, he decided to refound his old college, and the Italian Gothic of the two gateways is evidence of his delight in the style with which he had become familiar at Padua and elsewhere. He built the two wings of the Caius Court, leaving the Court open towards the south. The idea of his three gates, beginning with the simple Gate of Humility, leading to the Gate of Virtue, and so to that of Honour, is very fitting, for such sermons in stones could scarcely find a better place than in a university. Caius has many famous medical men, treasuring the memory of Harvey, who discovered the circulation of the blood, and of Dr. Butts, who was Henry VIII.'s physician.

TRINITY HALL.—As already mentioned, Trinity Hall was founded two years after Gonville made his modest foundation. It is specialized in relation to law as its neighbour is to medicine. Although architecturally of less account, its modern work is free from anything obtrusively out of keeping with academic tradition. Salvin's uninspired eastern side of the court containing the entrance was built after a fire in 1852, and is typical of his harsh and unsympathetic work. Behind the Georgian front of the north side of this court, there is a good deal of the fabric of the Tudor buildings, and some of the lecture-rooms, with their oak panelling and big chimneys, are most picturesque.

On the west side is the hall, dating from 1743, and the modern combination room, containing a curious old semi-circular table, with a counter-balance railway for passing the wine from one corner to the other. The chapel is on the south side, and is a few years earlier than the hall.

CORPUS CHRISTI.—Within two years from the founding of Trinity Hall Corpus Christi came into being, the gild of St. Benedict's Church, in conjunction with that of St. Mary the Great, having obtained a charter for this purpose from Edward III. in 1352, Henry Duke of Lancaster, the King's cousin, being alderman at that time.

This was the last of the colleges founded in the first period of college-building, and it has managed to preserve under the shadow of the Saxon tower of the parish church, which was for long the college chapel, one of the oldest and most attractive courts in Cambridge. Several of the windows and doors have been altered in later times, but otherwise three sides of the court are completely mediaeval. Having retained this fine relic, the college seems to have been content to let all the rest go, when, in 1823, Wilkins, whose bad Gothic we have seen at King's College, was allowed to rebuild the great court, including the chapel and hall. Sir Nicholas Bacon and Matthew Parker, Archbishop of Canterbury, are two of the most famous names associated with Corpus Christi. Parker left his old college a splendid collection of manuscripts, which are preserved in the library. This college has a strong ecclesiastical flavour, and it is therefore fitting that it should possess such a remarkable document as the original draft of the Thirty-nine Articles, which is among the treasured manuscripts.

QUEENS'.—After the founding of Corpus there came an interval of nearly a century before the eight colleges then existing were added to. Henry VI. founded King's in 1441, and seven years later his young Queen Margaret of Anjou, who was only eighteen, was induced by Andrew Docket to take over his very modest beginning in the way of a college. It was refounded under the name of Queen's College, having in the two previous years of its existence been dedicated to St. Bernard. As in the case of King's, the progress of Margaret's college was handicapped by the Wars of the Roses, but fortunately Edward IV.'s Queen, Elizabeth Woodville, espoused the cause of Margaret's college when Docket appealed to her for help.

Above all other memories this college glories in its associations with Erasmus, who was probably advised to go there by Bishop Fisher. There are certain of his letters extant which he dates from Queens', and it is interesting to find that he wrote in a querulous fashion of the bad wine and beer he had to drink when his friend Ammonius failed to send him his usual cask of the best Greek wine. He also complained of being beset by thieves, and being shut up because of plague, but it need not be thought from this that Cambridge was much worse than other places.

Of all the colleges in the University Queens' belongs most completely to other days. Its picturesque red brick entrance tower is the best of this type of gateway, which is such a distinctive feature of Cambridge, and the first court is similar to St. John's, with which Bishop Fisher was so closely connected as Lady Margaret Beaufort's executor. In the inner court, whose west front makes a charming picture from the river, is the President's Lodge occupying the north side. Its oriel windows and rough cast walls of quite jovial contours overhanging the dark cloisters beneath strike a different note to anything else in Cambridge. Restoration has altered the appearance of the hall since its early days, but it is an interesting building, with some notable portraits and good stained glass. The court, named after Erasmus, at the south-west angle of the college was, it is much to be regretted, rebuilt by Essex in the latter part of the eighteenth century; but for this the view of the river front from the curiously constructed footbridge would have been far finer than it is. Like the sundial in the first court, this bridge, leading to soft meadows beneath the shade of great trees, is attributed to Sir Isaac Newton.

ST. CATHERINE'S.—This college was founded in 1473 by Robert Woodlark, Chancellor of the University, and dedicated to "the glorious Virgin Martyr, St. Catherine of Alexandria." Undergraduate slang, alas! reduces all this to "Cat's." It was originally called St. Catherine's Hall, and is one of the smallest of the colleges. Although not claiming the strong ecclesiastical flavour of Corpus, it has educated quite a formidable array of bishops. From Trumpington Street the buildings have the appearance of a pleasant manor-house of Queen Anne or early Georgian days, and, with the exception of the wing at the north-west, the whole of the three-sided court dates between 1680 and 1755. Both chapel and hall are included in this period.

JESUS.—Standing so completely apart from the closely clustered nucleus, Jesus College might be regarded as a modern foundation ranking with Downing or Selwyn by the hurried visitor who had failed to consult his guide-book and had not previous information to aid him. It was actually founded as long ago as 1497, and the buildings include the church and other parts of the Benedictine nunnery of the Virgin and St. Rhadegund.

Bishop Alcock, of Ely, was the founder of the college, and his badge, composed of three cocks' heads, is frequently displayed on the buildings.

The entrance gate, dating from the end of the fifteenth century, with stepped parapets, is the work of the founder, and is one of the best features of the college. Passing through this Tudor arch, we enter the outer court, dating from the reign of Charles I., but finished in Georgian times. From this the inner court is entered, and here we are in the nuns' cloister, with their church, now the college chapel, to the south, and three beautiful Early English arches, which probably formed the entrance to the chapter-house, noticeable on the east. In this court are the hall, the lodge, and the library, but the most interesting of all the buildings is the chapel. It is mainly the Early English church of the nunnery curtailed and altered by Bishop Alcock, who put in Perpendicular windows and removed aides without a thought of the denunciations he has since incurred. In many of the windows the glass is by Morris and Burne-Jones, and the light that passes through them gives a rich and solemn dignity to the interior.

CHRIST'S.—Perhaps the most impressive feature of Christ's College is the entrance gate facing the busy shopping street called Petty Cury. The imposing heraldic display reminds us at once of Lady Margaret Beaufort, who, in 1505, refounded God's House, the hostel which had previously stood here. Although restored, the chapel is practically of the same period as the gateway, and it and the hall have both interesting interiors. From the court beyond, overlooked on one side by the fine classic building of 1642 attributed to Inigo Jones, entrance is gained to the beautiful fellows' garden, where the mulberry-tree associated with the memory of Milton may still be seen.

MAGDALENE.—This college is the only old one on the outer side of the river. It stands on the more historic part of Cambridge; but although an abbey hostel was here in Henry VI.'s time, it was not until 1542, after the suppression of Crowland Abbey, to which the property belonged, that Magdalene was founded by Thomas, Baron Audley of Walden. In the first court of ivy-grown red brick is the rather uninteresting chapel, and on the side facing the entrance the hall stands between the two courts. It has some interesting portraits, including one of Samuel Pepys, and a good double staircase leading to the combination room, but more notable than anything else is the beautiful Renaissance building in the inner court, wherein is preserved the library of books Pepys presented to his old college. In the actual glass-covered bookcases in which he kept them, and in the very order, according to size, that Pepys himself adopted, we may see the very interesting collection of books he acquired. Here, too, is the famous Diary, in folio volumes, of neatly written shorthand, and other intensely interesting possessions of the immortal diarist.

EMMANUEL.—The college stands on the site of a Dominican friary, but Sir Walter Mildmay, the founder, or his executors, being imbued with strong Puritanism, delighted in sweeping away the monastic buildings they found still standing. Ralph Symons was the first architect, but all his excellent Elizabethan work has vanished, the oldest portion of the college only dating back to 1633. From that time up to the end of the eighteenth century the rest of the structures were reconstructed in the successive styles of classic revival. Wren began the work, but unluckily it was left to Essex to complete it, and he is responsible for the dreary hall occupying the site of the old chapel.

SIDNEY SUSSEX.—At the foot of the list of post-Reformation colleges comes Sidney Sussex, founded, in 1589, by Frances Lady Sussex, daughter of Sir William Sidney, and widow of the second Earl of Sussex. During the mania for rebuilding, all the Elizabethan work of Ralph Symons was replaced by Essex, and in the nineteenth century the notorious Wyatville, whose Georgian Gothic removed all the glamour from Windsor Castle, finished the work.

DOWNING.—The remaining colleges belong to the period we may call recent. Downing, the first of these, was not a going concern until 1821, although Sir George Downing, the founder, made the will by which his property was eventually devoted to this purpose as early as the year 1717.

RIDLEY HALL came into being in 1879, and is an adjunct to the other colleges for those who have already graduated and have decided to enter the Church.

SELWYN COLLEGE, founded about the same time, is named after the great Bishop Selwyn, who died in 1877. The college aims at the provision, on a hostel basis, of a University education on a less expensive scale than the older colleges.

Of the two women's colleges, Girton was founded first. This was in 1869, and the site chosen was as far away as Hitchen, but four years later, gaining confidence, the college was moved to Girton, a mile north-west of the town, on the Roman Via Devana. Newnham arrived on the scene soon afterwards, and, considering proximity to the University town no disadvantage, the second women's college was planted between Ridley and Selwyn, with Miss Clough as the first principal.

CHAPTER V
THE UNIVERSITY LIBRARY, THE SENATE HOUSE, THE PITT PRESS, AND THE MUSEUMS

In the early days when the University of Cambridge was still in an embryonic state, the various newly formed communities of academic learning had no corporate centre whatever. "The chancellor and masters" are first mentioned in a rescript of Bishop Balsham dated 1276, eight years before he founded Peterhouse, the first college, and six years before this Henry III. had addressed a letter to "the masters and scholars of Cambridge University," so that between these two dates it would appear that the chancellor really became the prime academic functionary. But it was not until well into the fourteenth century that any University buildings made their appearance.

The "schools quadrangle" was begun when Robert Thorpe, knight, was chancellor (1347-64), and during the following century various schools for lecturing and discussions on learned matters were built round the court, now entirely devoted to the library. Unfortunately, the medieval character of these buildings has been masked by a classic façade on the south, built in 1754, when it was thought necessary to make the library similar in style to the newly built Senate House. Thus without any further excuse the fine Perpendicular frontage by Thomas Rotherham, Bishop of Lincoln and fellow of King's, was demolished to make way for what can only be called a most unhappy substitute. George I. was really the cause of this change, for in 1715 he presented Cambridge with Dr. John Moore's extensive library, and not having the space to accommodate the little Hanoverian's gift, the authorities decided to add the old Senate House, which occupied the north side of the quadrangle, to the library, and to build a new Senate House; and the building then erected, designed by Mr., afterwards Sir James, Burrough, is still in use. It is a well-proportioned and reposeful piece of work, although the average undergraduate probably has mixed feelings when he gazes at the double line of big windows between composite pillasters supporting the rather severe cornice. For in this building, in addition to the "congregations," or meetings, of the Senate consisting of resident and certain non-resident masters of art, the examinations for degrees were formerly held. Here on the appointed days, early in the year, the much-crammed undergraduates passed six hours of feverish writing, and here, ten days later, in the midst of a scene of long-established disorder, their friends heard the results announced. Immediately the name of the Senior Wrangler was given out there was a pandemonium of cheering, shouting, yelling, and cap-throwing, and the same sort of thing was repeated until the list of wranglers was finished. Following this, proctors threw down from the oaken galleries printed lists of the other results, and a wild struggle at once took place in which caps and gowns were severely handled, and for a time the marble floor was covered with a fighting mob of students all clutching at the fluttering papers, while the marble features of the two first Georges, William Pitt, and the third Duke of Somerset remained placidly indifferent.

Although there is no space here to describe the many early books the library contains, it is impossible to omit to mention that among the notable manuscripts exhibited in the galleries is the famous *Codex Bezae* presented to the University by Theodore Beza, who rescued it, in 1562, when the monastery at Lyons, in which it was preserved, was being destroyed. This manuscript is in uncial letters on vellum in Greek and Latin, and includes the four Gospels and the Acts.

It was a pardonable mistake for the old-time "freshman" to think the Pitt Press in Trumpington Street was a church, but no one does this now, because the gate tower, built about 1832, when the Gothic revival was sweeping the country, is now known as "the Freshman's Church." The Pitt Press was established with a part of the fund raised to commemorate William Pitt, who was educated at Pembroke College nearly opposite.

The University Press publishes many books, and gives special attention to books the publication of which tends to the advancement of learning. The two Universities and the King's printer have still a monopoly in printing the Bible and Book of Common Prayer.

The magnificent museum founded by Richard, Viscount Fitzwilliam, is a little farther down Trumpington Street. It was finished in 1847 by Cockerell, who added the unhappy north side to the University Library, but the original architect was Basevi, who was prevented from finishing the building he had begun by his untimely death through falling from one of the towers of Ely Cathedral. The magnificence of the great portico, with its ceiling of encrusted ornament, is vastly impressive, but the marble staircase in the entrance lobby, with its rich crimson reds, is rather overpowering in conjunction with the archaeological exhibits. Plainer, cooler and less aggressive marble such as that employed in the lobby of the Victoria and Albert Museum would have been more suitable. A very considerable proportion of the museum's space is devoted to the collection of pictures—some of them copies—which the University has gathered. The interesting Turner water-colours presented by John Ruskin are here, with a Murillo, reputed to be his earliest known work, and a good many other examples of the work of famous men of the Italian and Dutch Schools.

Besides the Museum of Archaeology, between Peterhouse and the river, the vigorous growth of the scientific side of the University is shown in the vast buildings newly erected on both sides of Downing Street, which has now become a street of laboratories and museums. Now that the outworks of the hoary citadel of Classicism have been stormed, and the undermining of the great walls has already begun, the development of modern science at Cambridge will be accelerated, and in the face of the urgency of the demands of worldwide competition it would appear that the University on the Cam is more fitted to survive than her sister on the Isis.

CHAPTER VI
THE CHURCHES IN THE TOWN

Almost everyone who goes to Cambridge as a visitor bent on sightseeing naturally wishes to see the colleges before anything else, but it should not be forgotten that there are at least two churches, apart from the college chapels, whose importance is so great that to fail to see them would be a criminal omission. There are other churches of considerable interest, but for a description of them it is unfortunately impossible to find space.

Foremost in point of antiquity comes St. Benedict's, or St Benet's, possessing a tower belonging to pre-Conquest times, and the only structural relic of the Saxon town now in existence. The church was for a considerable time the chapel of Corpus Christi, and the ancient tower still rises picturesquely over the roofs of the old court of that college.

Without the tower, the church would be of small interest, for the nave and chancel are comparatively late, and have been rather drastically restored. The interior, nevertheless, is quite remarkable in possessing a massive Romanesque arch opening into the tower, with roughly carved capitals to its tall responds. Outside there are all the unmistakable features of Saxon work—the ponderously thick walls, becoming thinner in the upper parts, the "long and short" method of arranging the coigning, and the double windows divided with a heavy baluster as at Wharram-le-Street in Yorkshire, Earl's Barton in Northamptonshire, and elsewhere.

Next in age and importance to St. Benedict's comes what is popularly called "the Round Church," one of the four churches of the Order of Knights Templar now standing in this country. The other three are the Temple Church in London, St. Sepulchre's at Northampton, and Little Maplestead Church in Essex, and they are given in chronological order, Cambridge possessing the oldest. It was consecrated the Church of the Holy Sepulchre, and was built before the close of the eleventh century, and is therefore a work of quite early Norman times. The interior is wonderfully impressive, for it has nothing of the lightness and grace of the Transitional work in the Temple, and the heavy round arches opening into the circular aisle are supported by eight massive piers. Above there is another series of eight pillars, very squat, and of about the same girth as those below, and the spaces between are subdivided by a small pillar supporting two semi-circular arches. Part of the surrounding aisle collapsed in 1841, and the Cambridge Camden Society (now defunct) employed the architect Salvin to thoroughly restore the church. He took down a sort of battlemented superstructure erected long after the Norman period, and built the present conical roof.

After these early churches, the next in interest is Great St. Mary's, the University Church, conspicuously placed in the market-place and in the very centre of the town. It has not, however, always stood forth in such distinguished isolation, for only as recently as the middle of last century did the demolition take place of the domestic houses that surrounded it. And inside, the alterations in recent times have been quite as drastic, robbing the church of all the curious and remarkable characteristics it boasted until well past the middle of the nineteenth century, and reducing the whole interior to the stereotyped features of an average parish church.

If we enter the building to-day without any knowledge of its past, we merely note a spacious late Perpendicular nave, having galleries in the aisles with fine dark eighteenth-century panelled fronts, and more woodwork of this plain and solemn character in front of the organ, in the aisle chapels, and elsewhere. A soft greenish light from the clerestory windows (by Powell), with their rows of painted saints, falls upon the stonework of the arcades and the wealth of dark oak, but nothing strikes us as unusual until we discover that the pulpit is on rails, making it possible to draw it from the north side to a central position beneath the chancel arch. This concession to tradition is explained when we discover the state of the church before 1863, when Dr. Luard, who was then vicar, raised an agitation, before which the Georgian glories of the University Church passed away. Before the time of Laud, when so many departures from mediaeval custom had taken place, we learn, from information furnished during the revival brought about by the over-zealous archbishop, that the church was arranged much on the lines of a theatre, with a pulpit in the centre, which went by the name of the Cockpit, that the service was cut as short as "him that is sent thither to read it" thought fit, and that during sermon-time the chancel was filled with boys and townsmen "all in a rude heap between the doctors and the altar." But this concentration on the University sermon and disrespect for the altar went further, for, with the legacy of Mr. William Worts, the existing galleries were put up in 1735, the Cockpit was altered, and other changes made which Mr. A.H. Thompson has vividly described:

> … the centre of the church was filled with an immense
> octagonal pulpit on the "three-decker" principle, the
> crowning glory and apex of which was approached,

like a church-tower, by an internal staircase. About 1740
Burrough filled the chancel-arch and chancel with a
permanent gallery, which commanded a thorough view
of this object. The gallery, known as the "Throne," was
an extraordinary and unique erection. The royal family of
Versailles never worshipped more comfortably than did
the Vice-Chancellor and heads of houses, in their beautiful
armchairs, and the doctors sitting on the tiers of seats
behind them. In this worship of the pulpit, the altar was
quite disregarded…. The church thus became an oblong
box, with the organ at the end, the Throne at the other, and
the pulpit between them.

Of all this nothing remains besides the organ and the side galleries, and
of the splendid screen, built in 1640 to replace its still finer predecessor,
swept away by Archbishop Parker nearly a century before, only that portion
running across the north chapel remains.

Until the Senate House was built, the commencements were held in the
church, but thereafter it would appear that the sermon flourished almost to
the exclusion of anything else.

The diminutive little church of St. Peter near the Castle mound is of
Transitional Norman date, and has Roman bricks built into its walls.

> O fairest of all fair places,
>   Sweetest of all sweet towns!
> With the birds and the greyness and greenness,
>   And the men in caps and gowns.
>
> All they that dwell within thee,
>   To leave are ever loth,
> For one man gets friends, and another
>   Gets honour, and one gets both.

AMY LEVY: *A Farewell.*

INDEX

Edward VII.
Elizabeth, Queen
Elizabeth Woodville, Queen
Ely
Emmanuel College
Erasmus
Essex, James

Fisher, Bishop

George I.
Gibbs, James
Girton
Gonville, Edmund de
Gonville Hall
Grantchester
Great St. Mary's Church

Henry I.
Henry III.
Henry IV.
Henry VI.
Henry VII.
Henry VIII.
Hereward the Wake

Jesus College
Jones, Inigo

King's College
King's Hall

Magdalene College
Margaret of Anjou, Queen
Mary, Queen
Michael House
Mildmay, Sir Walter
Moore, Dr. John

Nevile, Thomas
Newnham
Newton, Sir Isaac

Parker, Archbishop
Parker, Matthew, Archbishop of Canterbury
Pembroke College
Pepys, Samuel
Perne, Dr. Andrew
Perse, Dr.
Peterhouse
Philip and Mary
Pitt Press
Pitt, William

Queens' College

Richard III.
Rickman, Thomas
Ridley Hall
Roman Cambridge
Round Church, The

St. Benedict's Church
St. Catherine's College
St. John's College
St. John's Hospital
St. Mary the Less
St. Peter's Church
Salvin, Anthony
Scott, Sir Gilbert
Selwyn College
Senate House
Sidney, Sir William
Sidney Sussex College
Skeat, Professor
Stourbridge Fair
Sussex, Frances Lady
Symons, Ralph

Tennyson, Lord
Thirty-nine Articles
Trinity College
Trinity Hall

Valance, Aymer de
Via Devana

Walpole, Sir Robert
Whewell, William
Wilberforce, William
Wilkins, William
William the Conqueror
Williams, Lord Keeper
Wordsworth, William
Wren, Bishop Matthew
Wren, Sir Christopher
Wyatville, Sir J.
Wykeham, William of

www.ingramcontent.com/pod-product-compliance
Lightning Source LLC
LaVergne TN
LVHW041805190726
843493LV00008B/2796